pensées

pensées

Romain Renault

The Onslaught Press

Published in Oxford by The Onslaught Press
11 Ridley Road, OX4 2QJ
August, 2015

Images © 2015 Romain Renault
Introduction © 2015 Yahia Lababidi

ISBN-13 978-0-9927238-6-6

Typeset in Le Monde Livre & Le Monde Sans,
& designed by Mathew D. Staunton

Printed by Lightning Source

Romain Renault is an idea man.

In his deceptively slight *pensées*, Renault muses out-loud in a series of illustrated epigrams. With enviable economy and mordant wit, he touches on matters absurd, philosophical, moral, psychological, or political. His terse, arresting visual aphorisms register, alternately, as micro-essays, a text book of wisecracks or, more broadly, exercises in seeing and thinking, differently. Whether accompanied by text or not, these clever reflections invite the reader/viewer to bring their own imagination, and mull over their swift performances, well after they've turned the page.

Like all good art, his *pensées* rewards repeated visiting. Ultimately, what emerges is a savage indictment of our self-defeating modern world and, past the well-deserved scolding, a call to action to right our wrongs. These razor-edged barbs are meant to shock us into living with more awareness and compassion.

Yahia Lababidi, Washington DC, August 2015

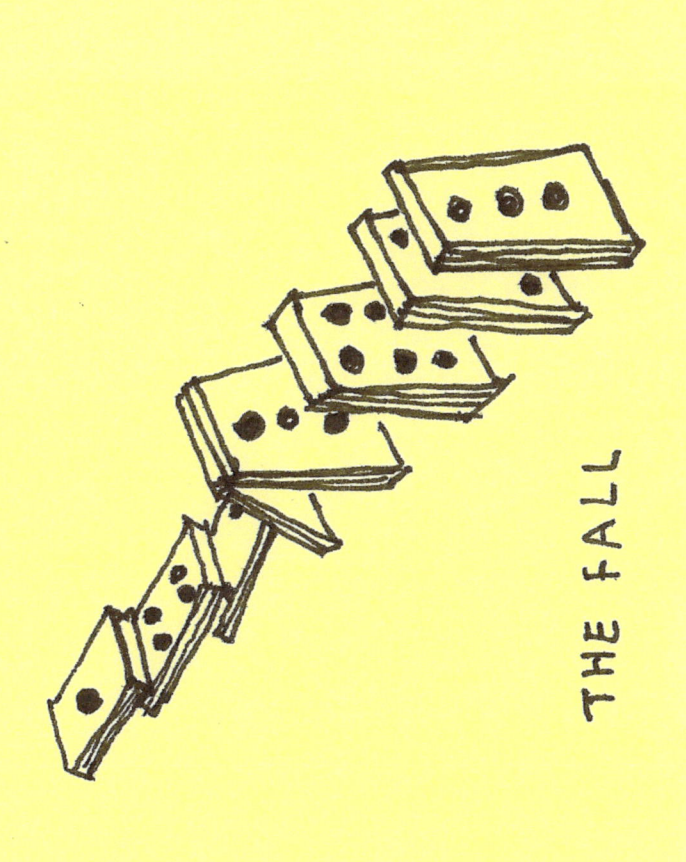

THE FALL

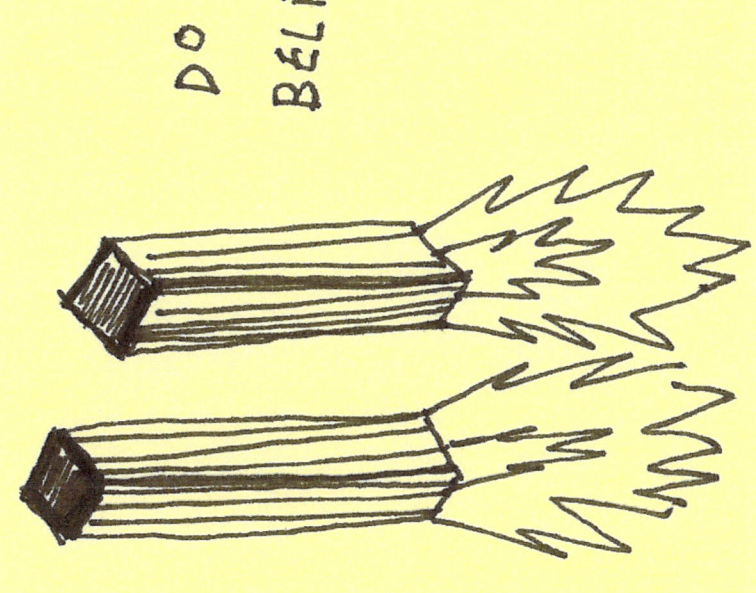

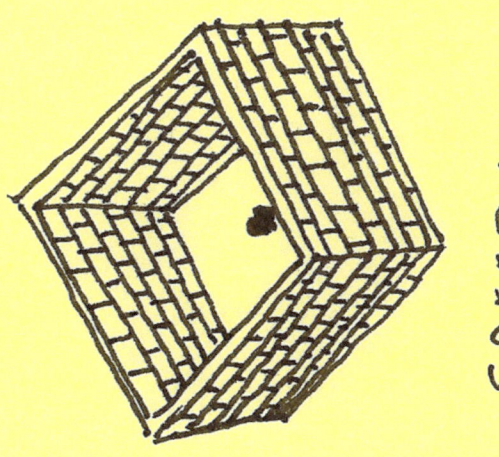

SAFETY

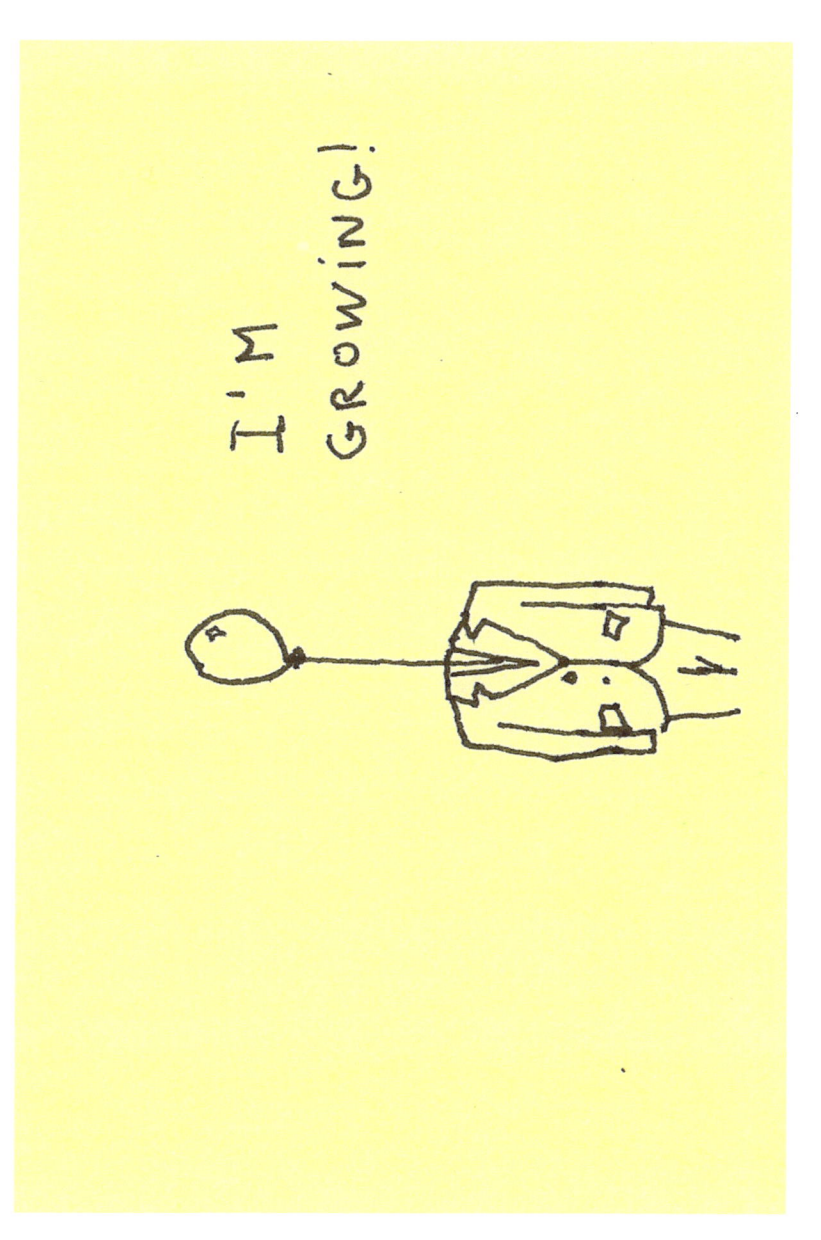

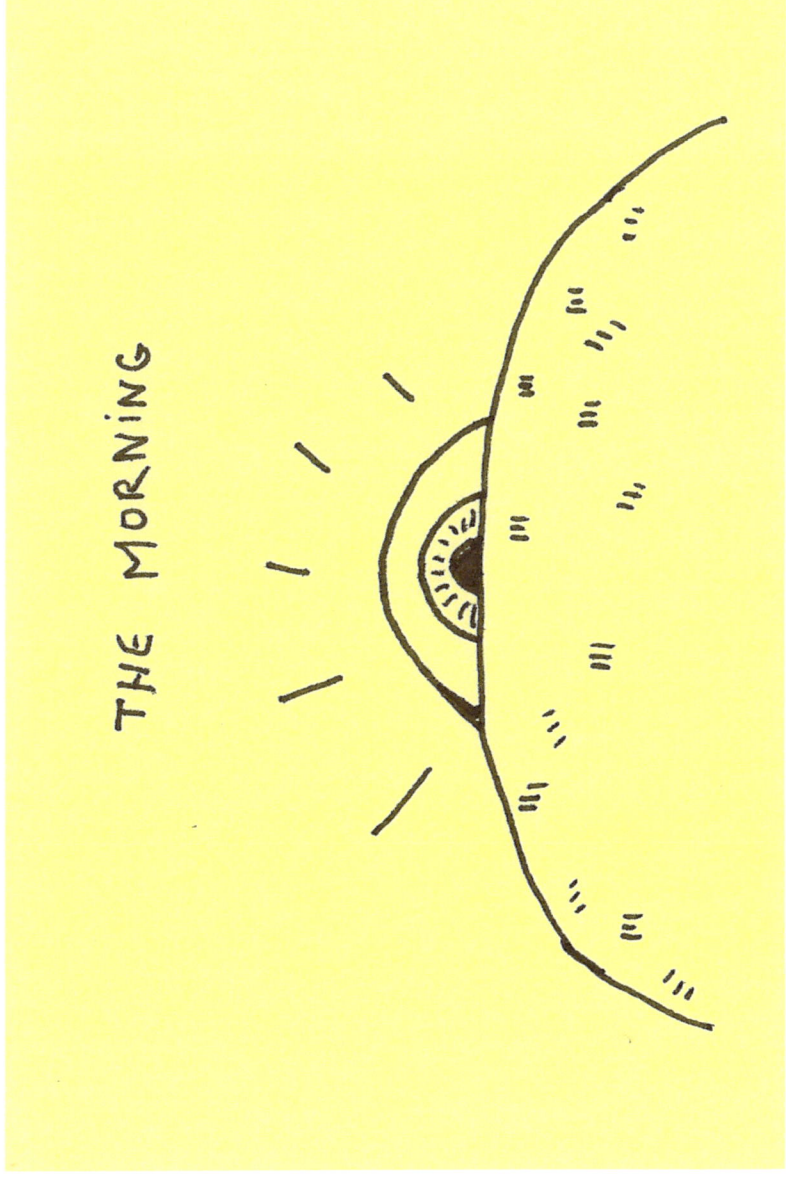

You say the truth is inside?

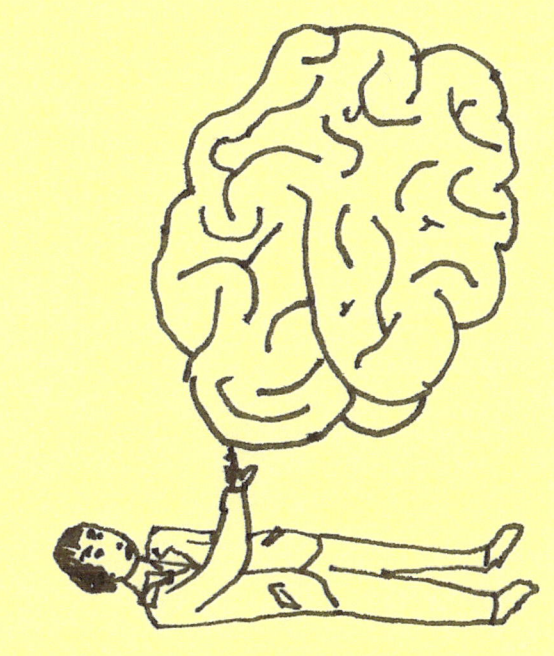

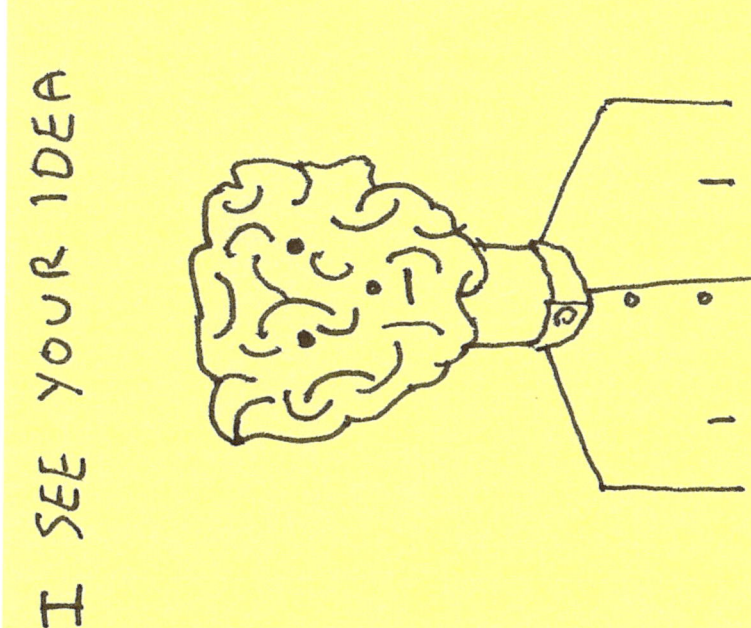

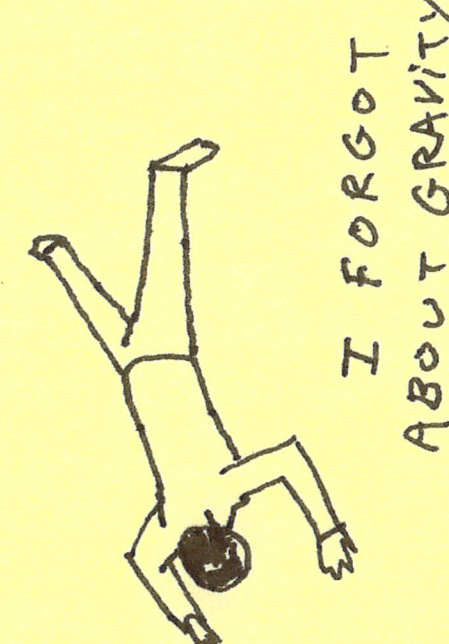

I FORGOT ABOUT GRAVITY

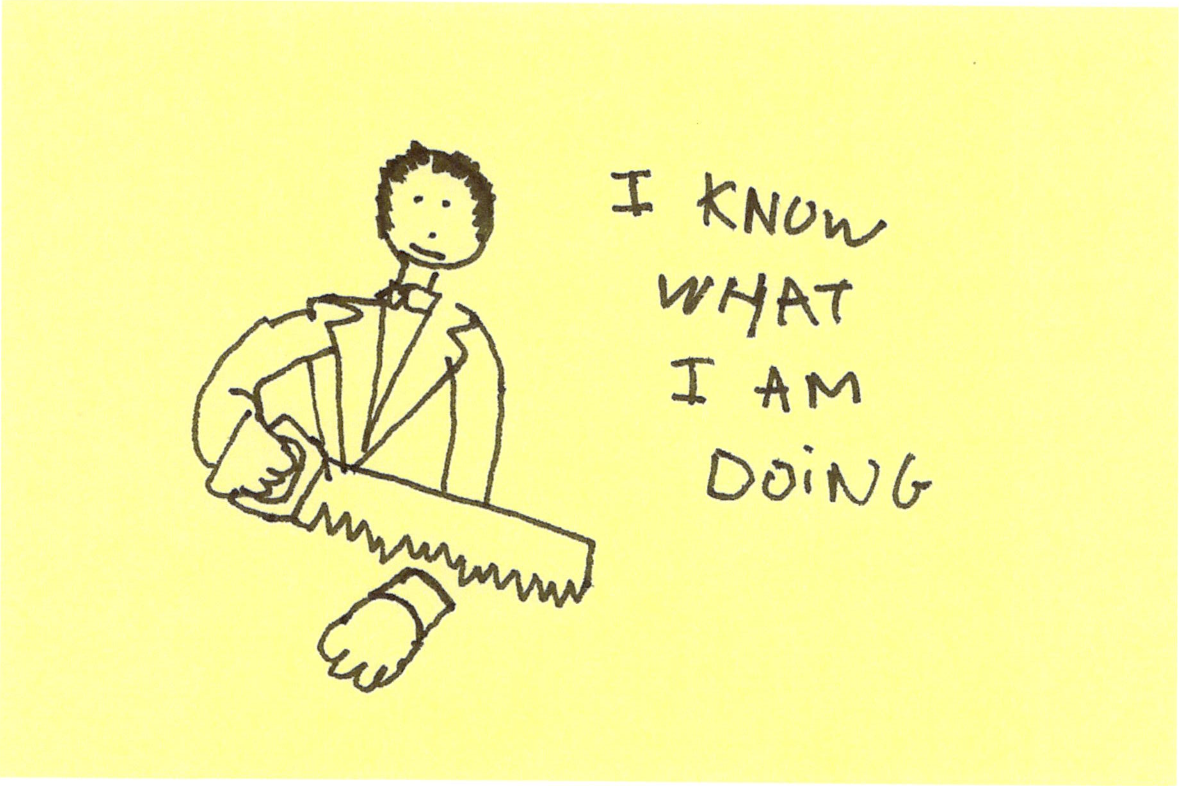
I KNOW
WHAT
I AM
DOING

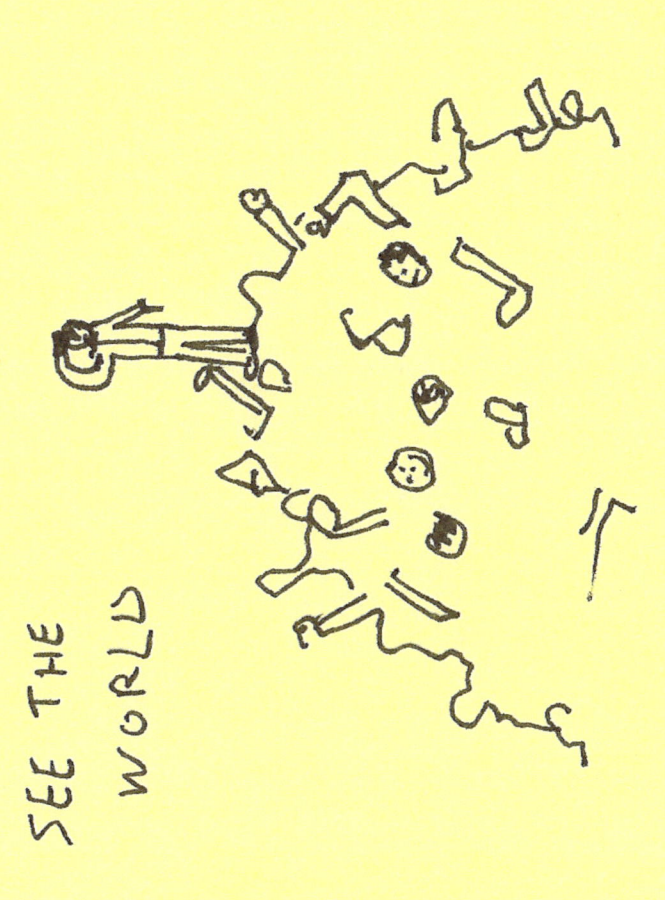

SEE THE
WORLD

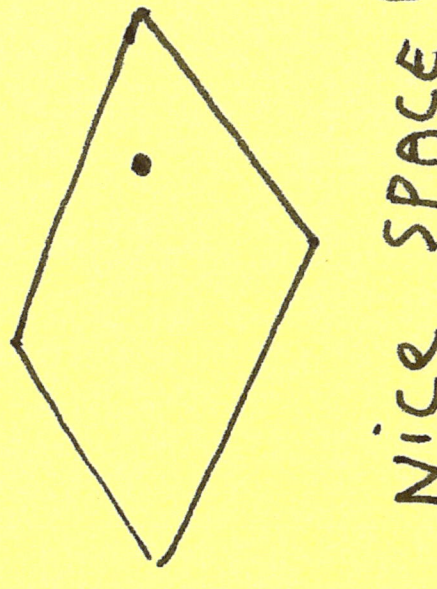

Nice Space!

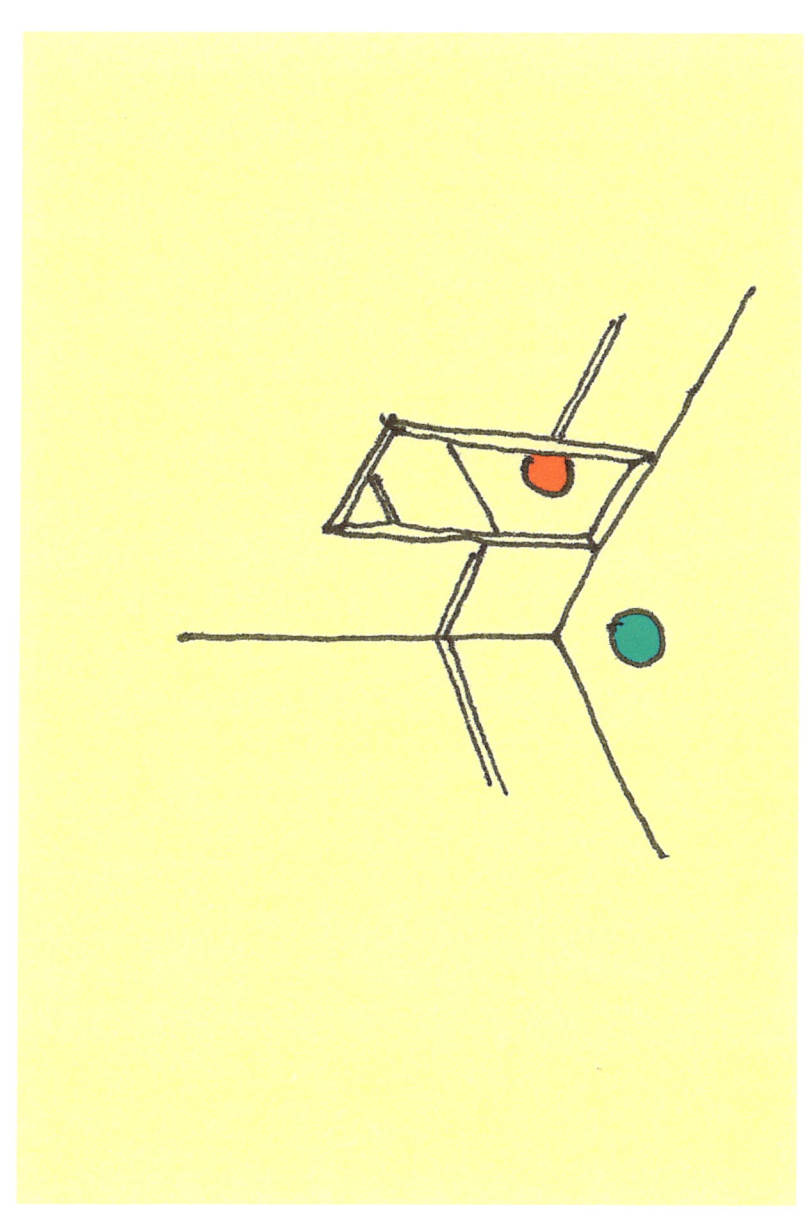

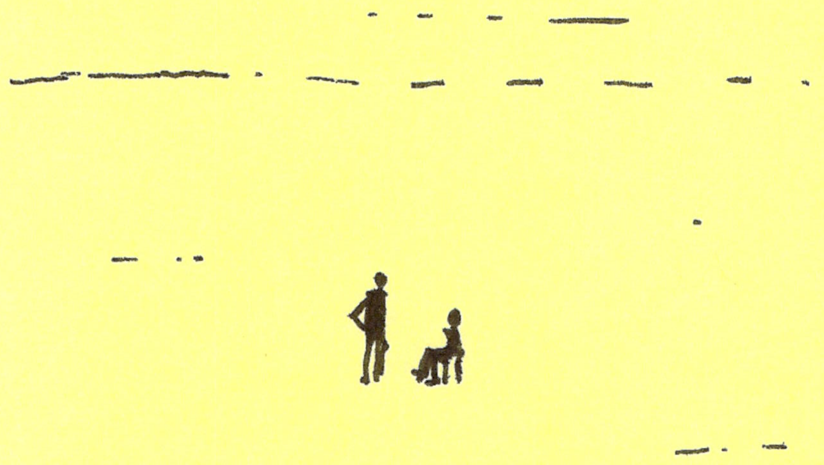

CAN I HAVE YOUR SEAT?

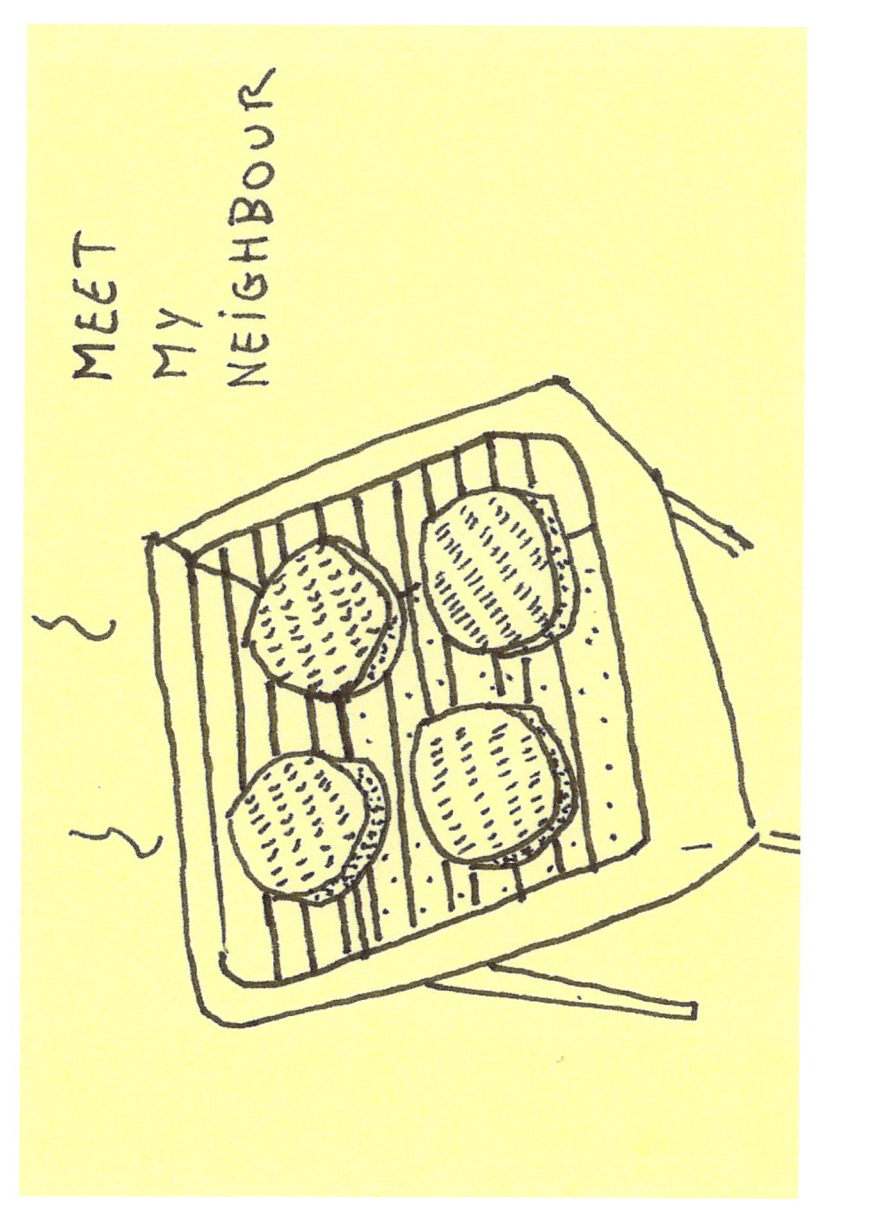

LIKE A FISH TO WATER

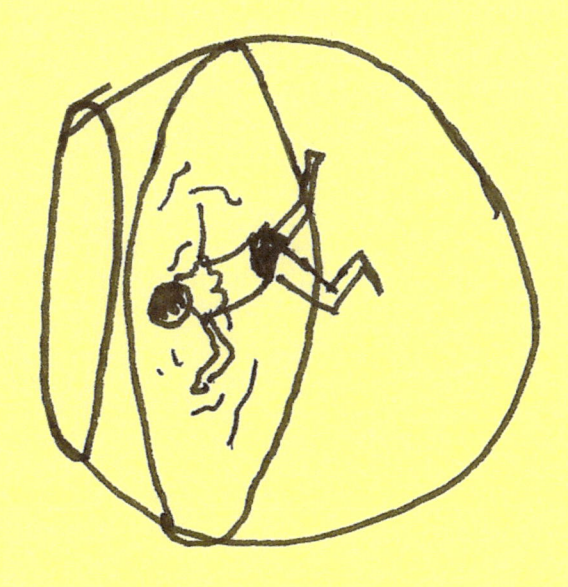

YOU CAN RUN BUT YOU CAN'T HIDE

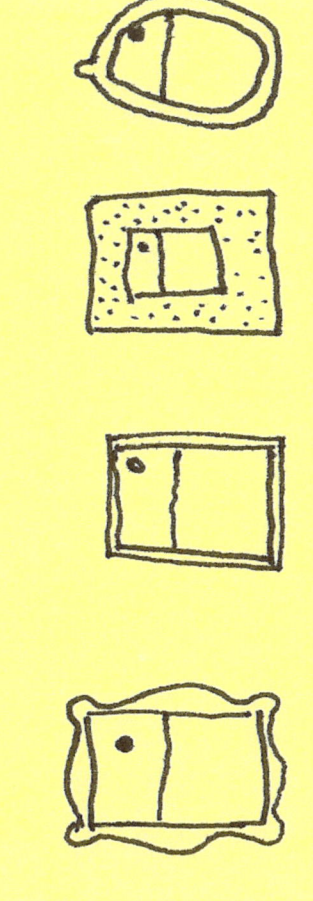

THINGS ARE NOT THE SAME

THIS IS NOT RIGHT

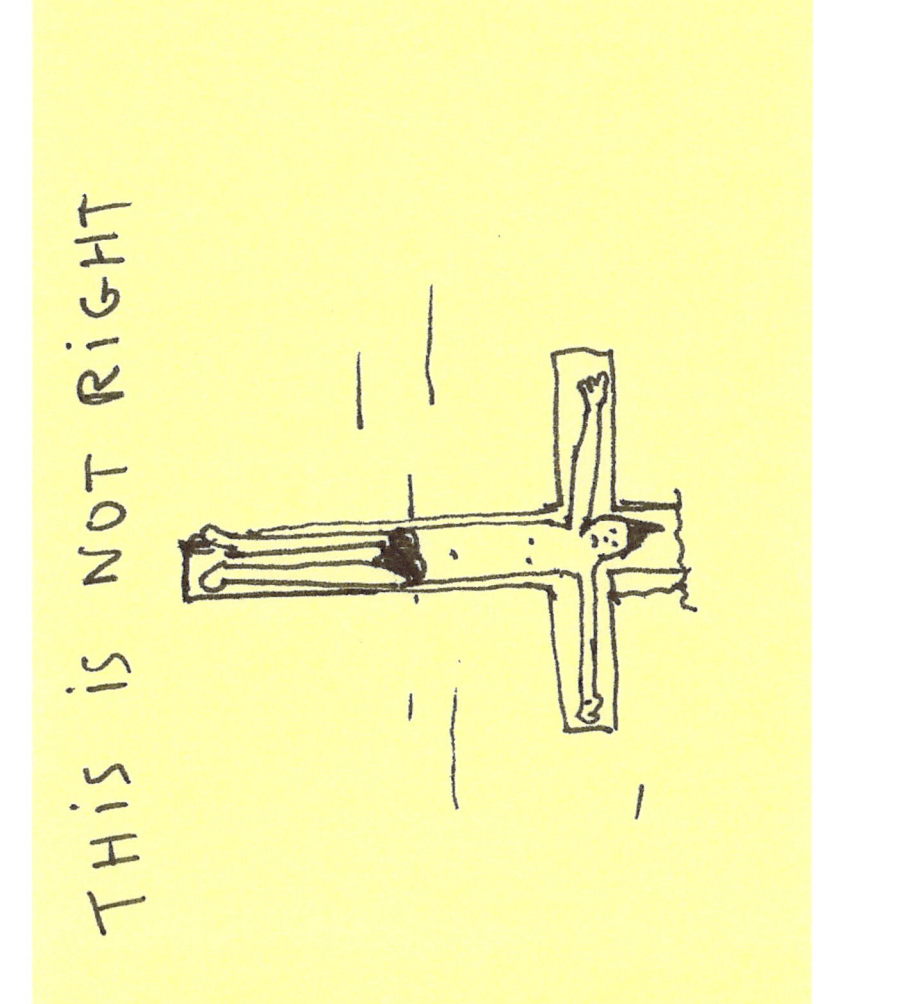

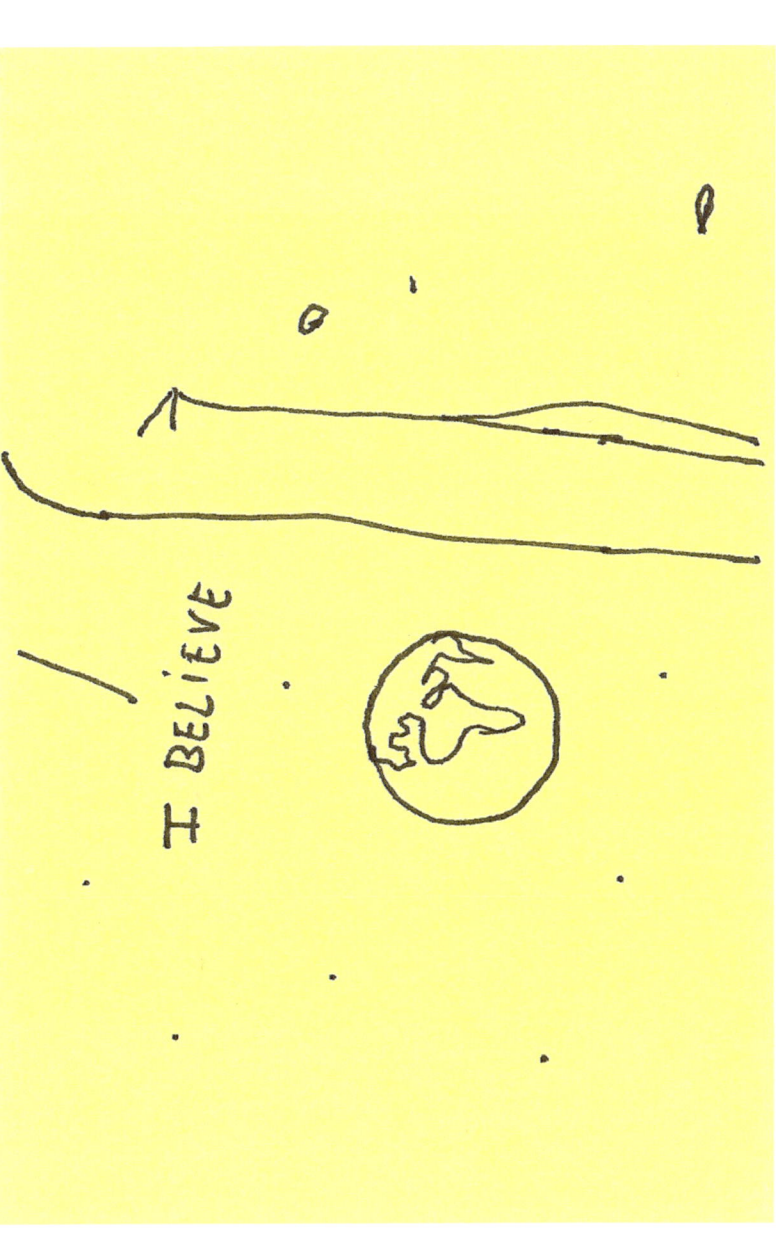

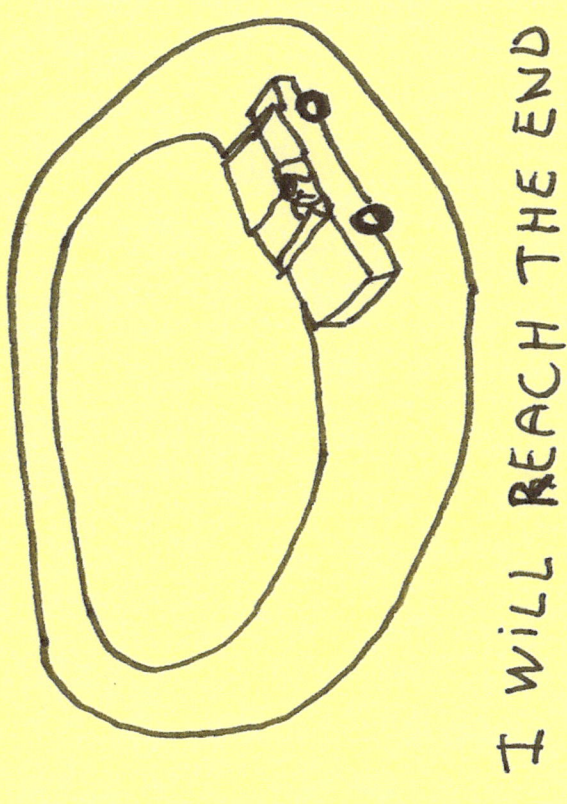

I WILL REACH THE END

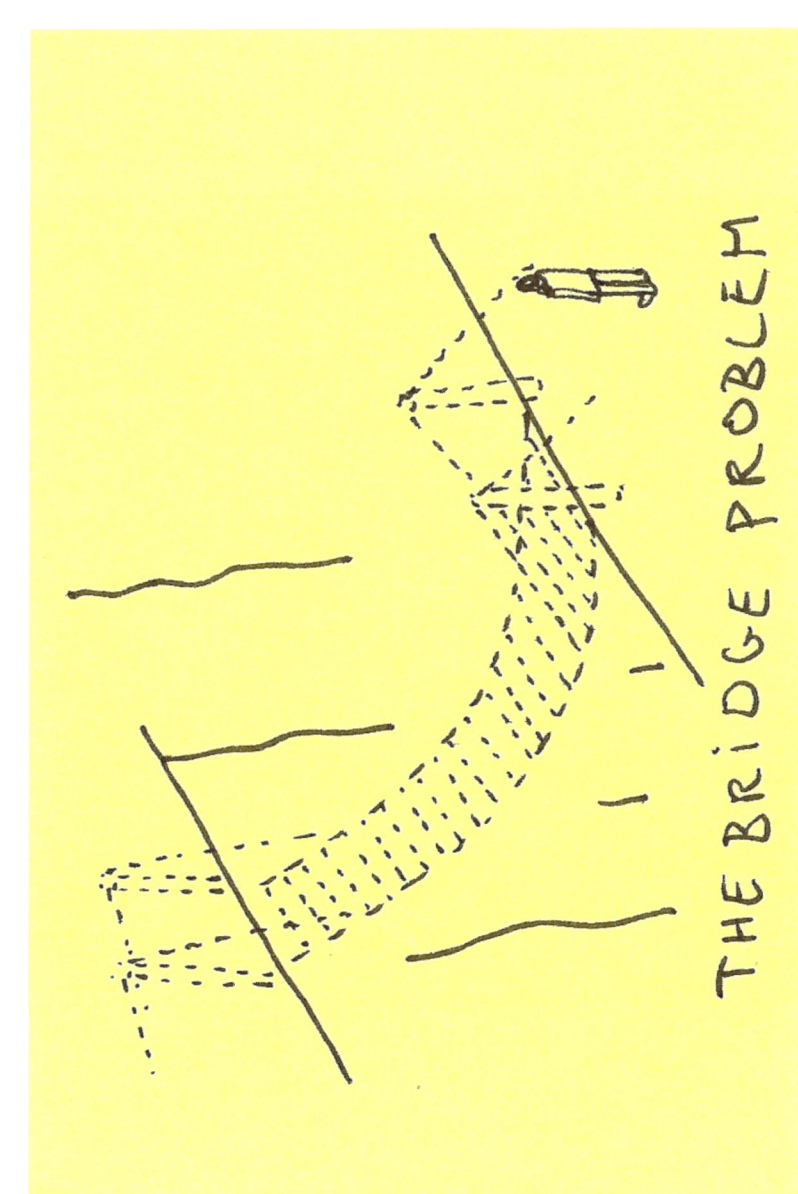

THE BRIDGE PROBLEM

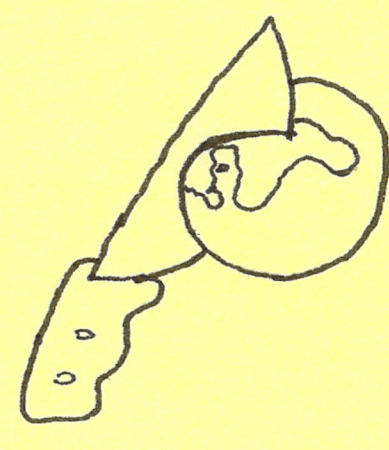

WILL YOU HAVE A SHARE?

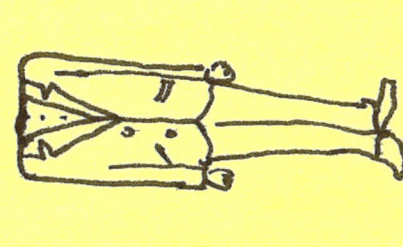

I TOOK OFF WHAT I DON'T NEED

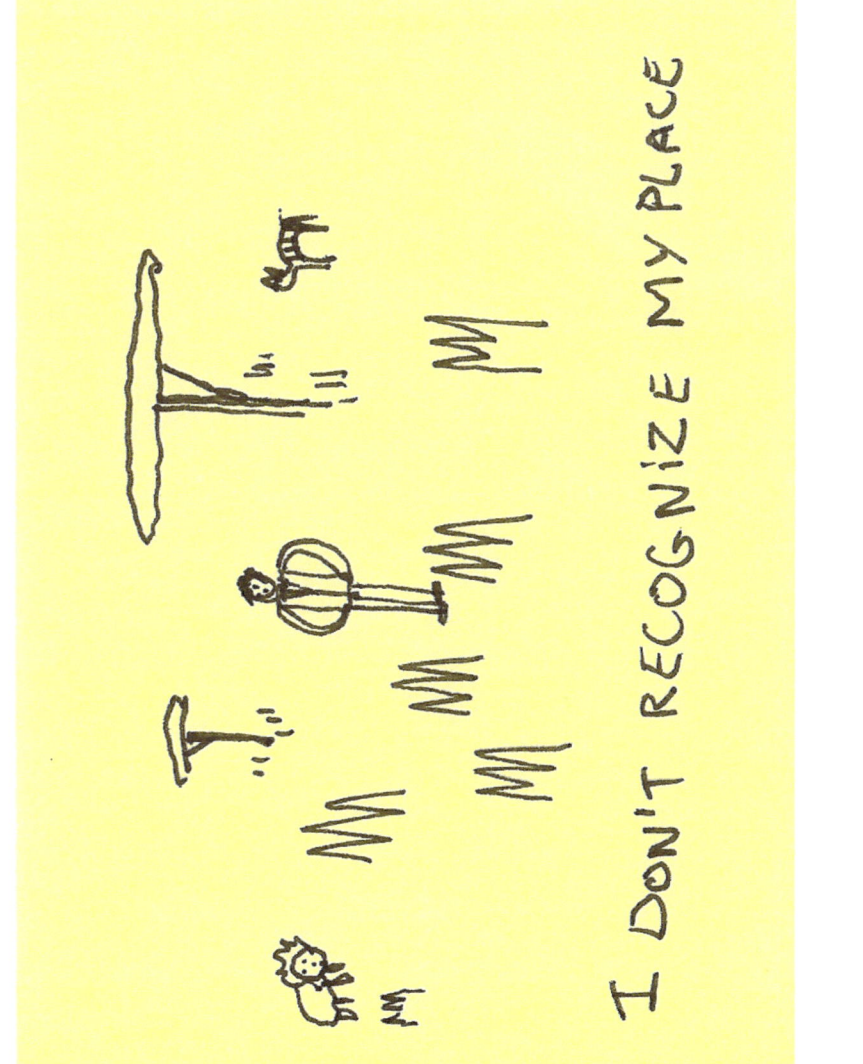

I DON'T RECOGNIZE MY PLACE

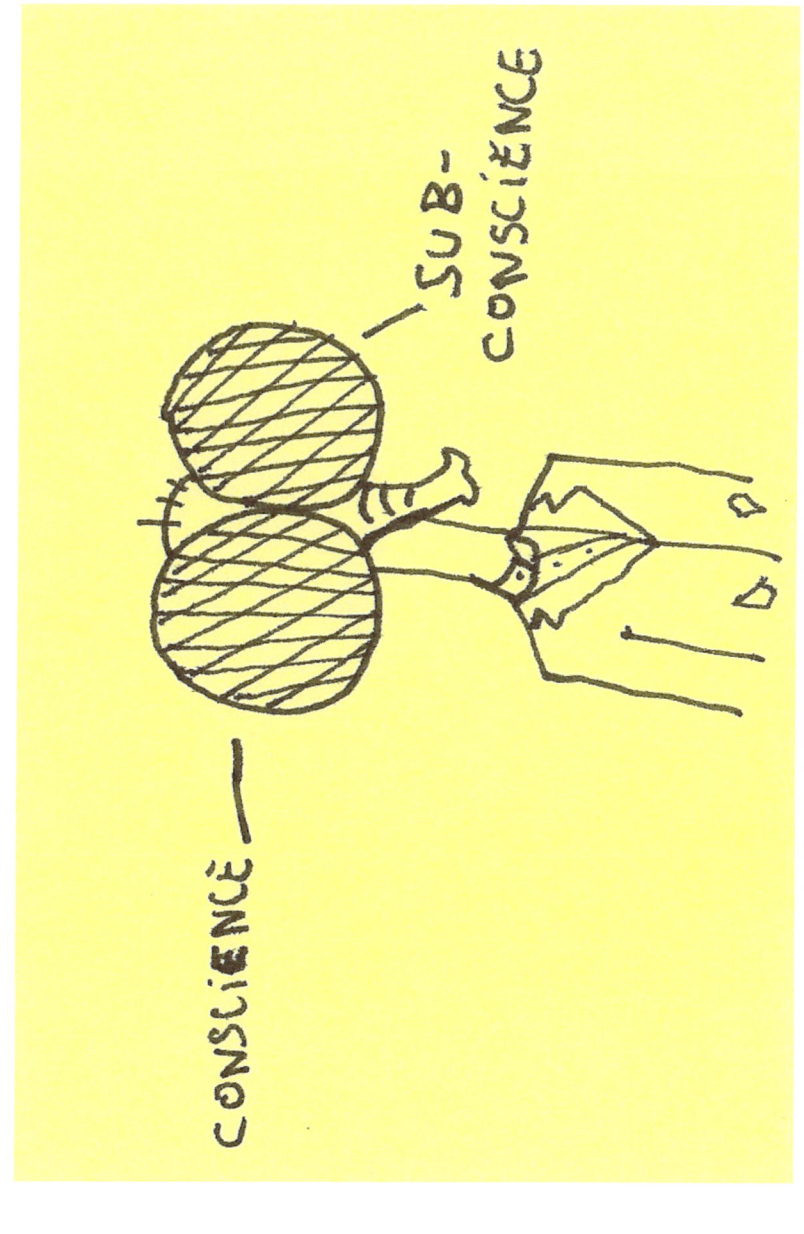

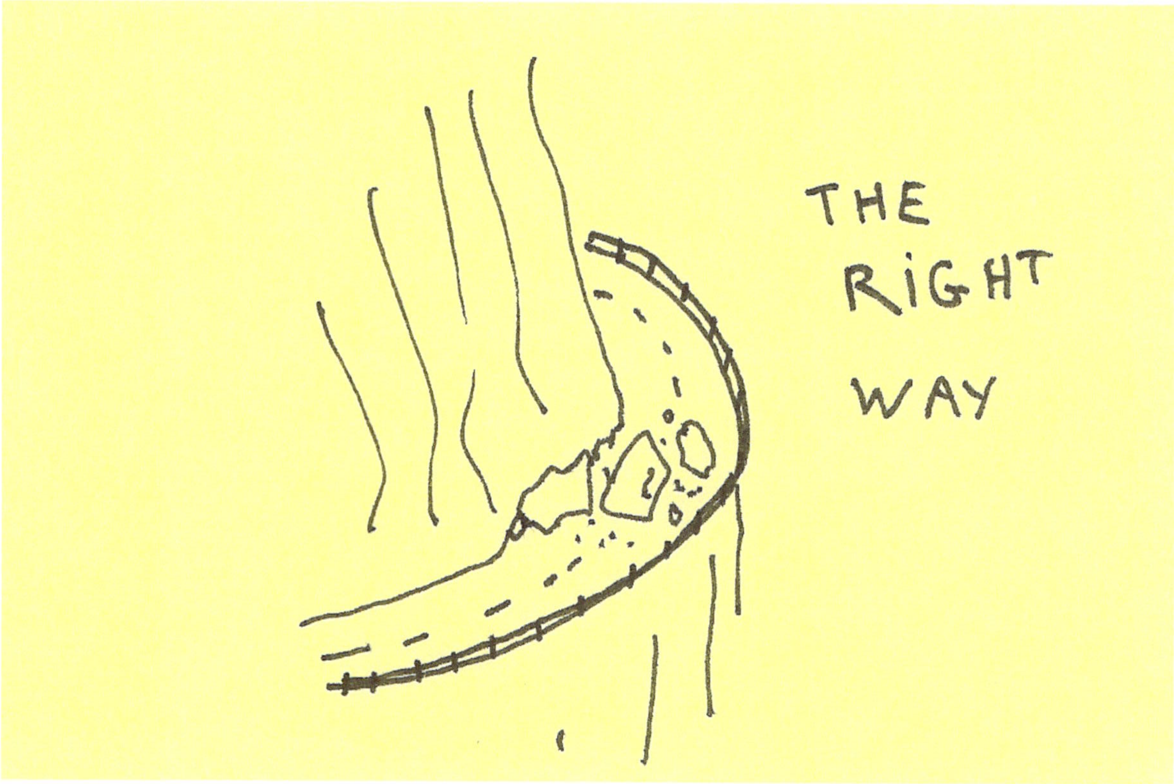
THE
RIGHT
WAY

I KNEW
WE WOULD
MEET

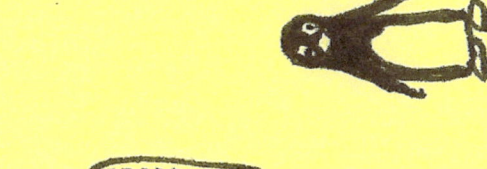
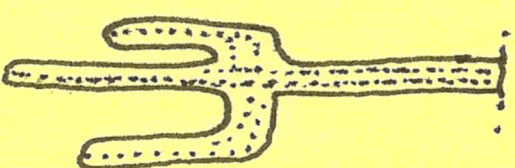

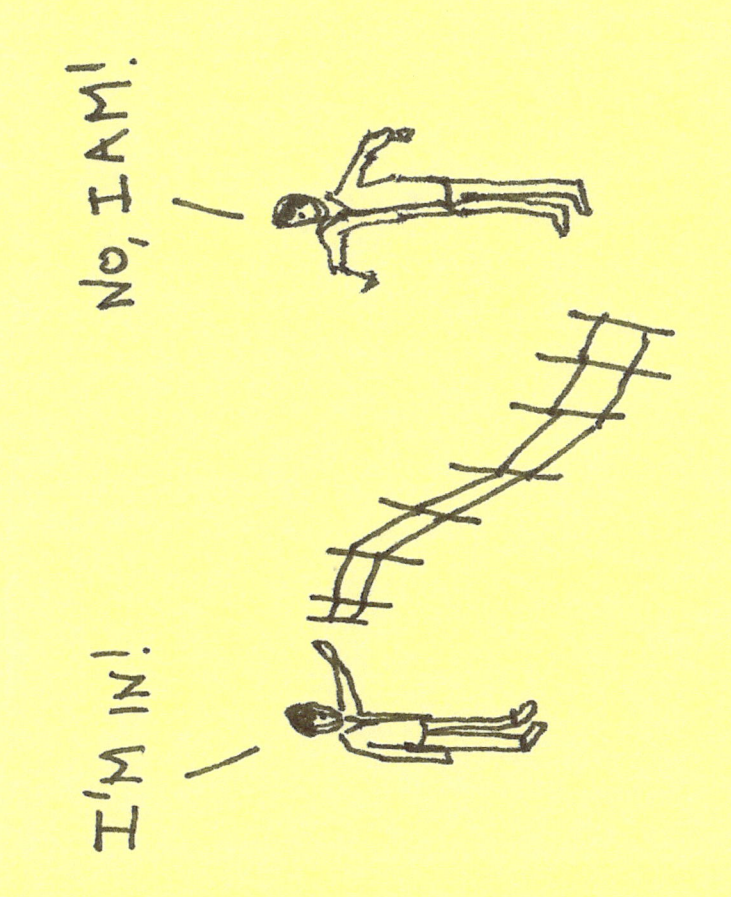

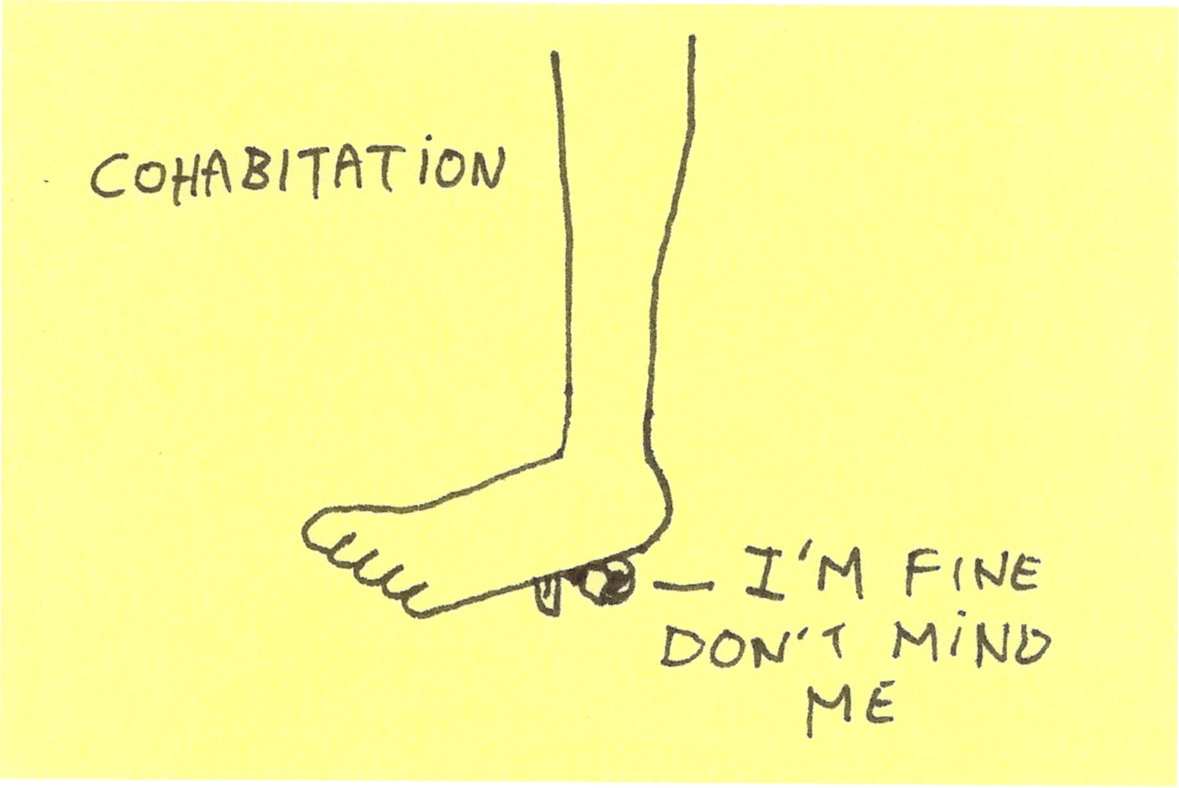
COHABITATION
I'M FINE DON'T MIND ME

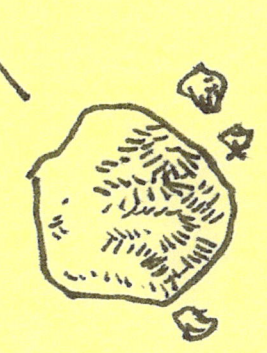

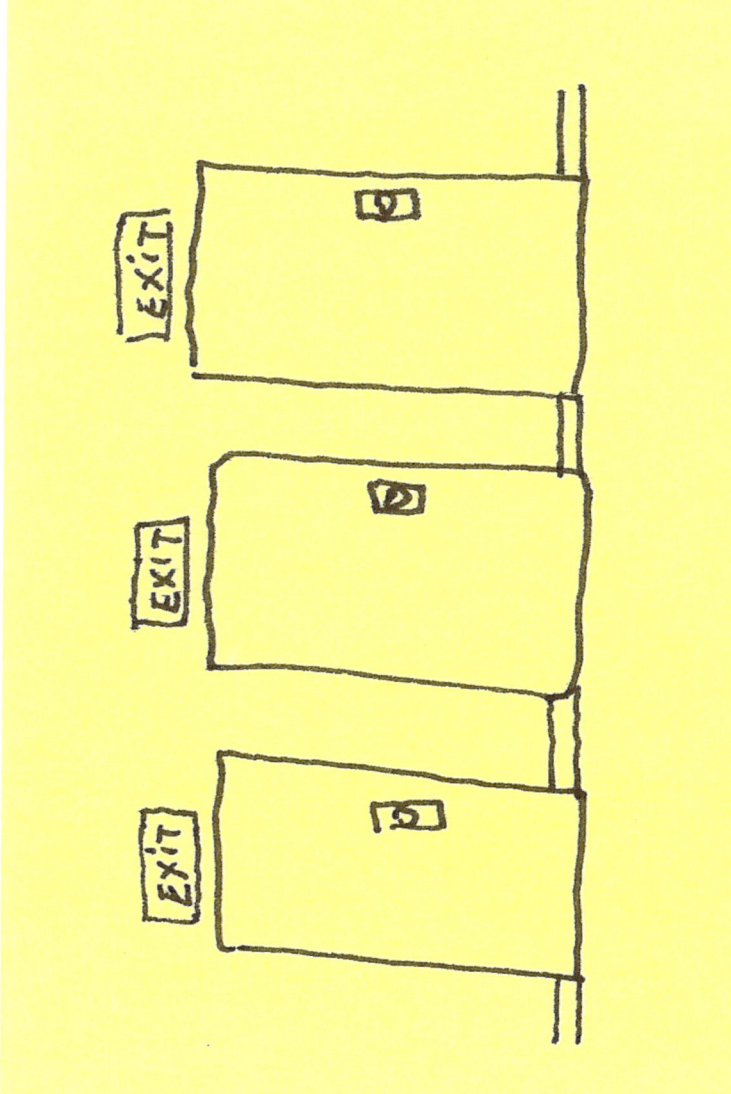

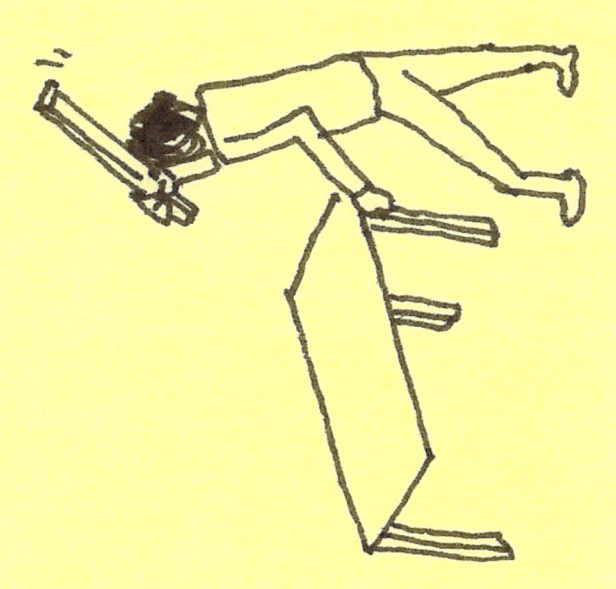

THE SECRET GARDEN KEEPER

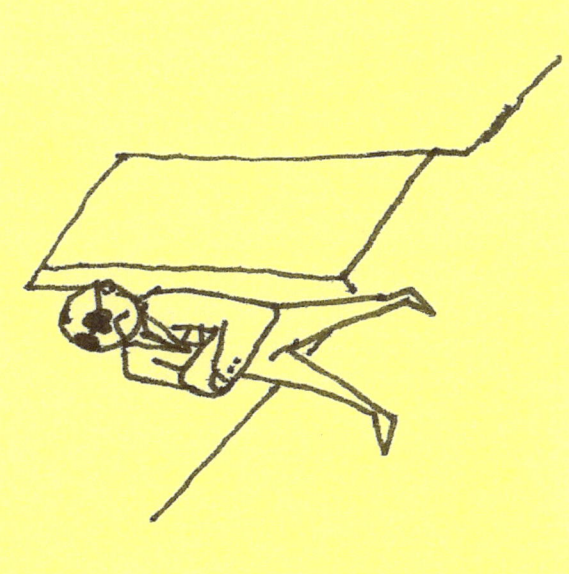

COME ON! GO GET IT!

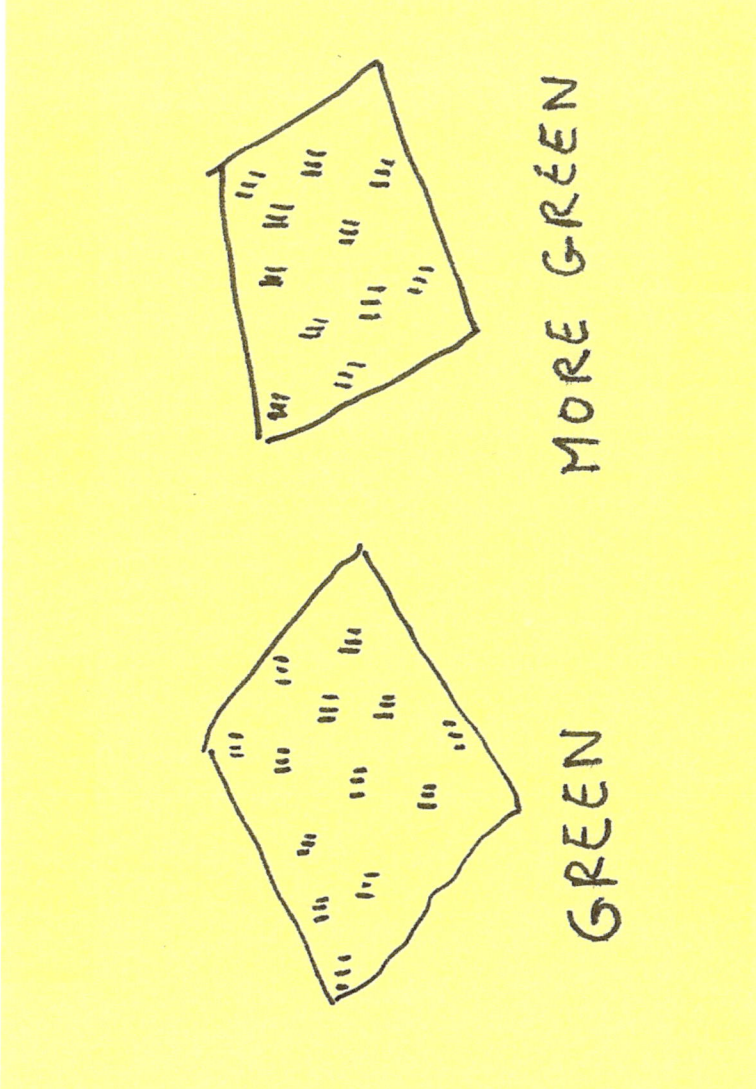

MORE GREEN

GREEN

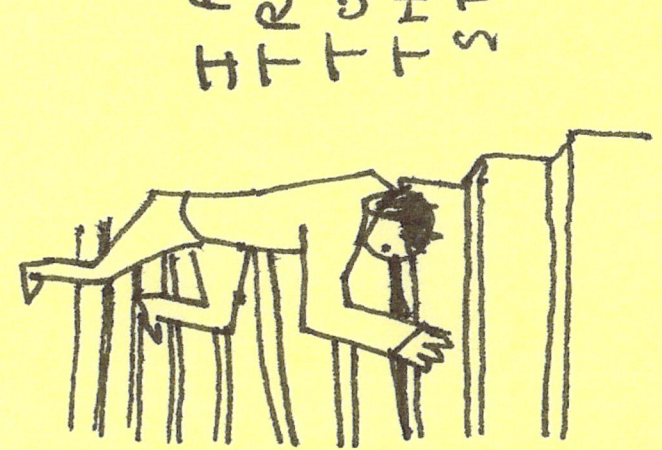

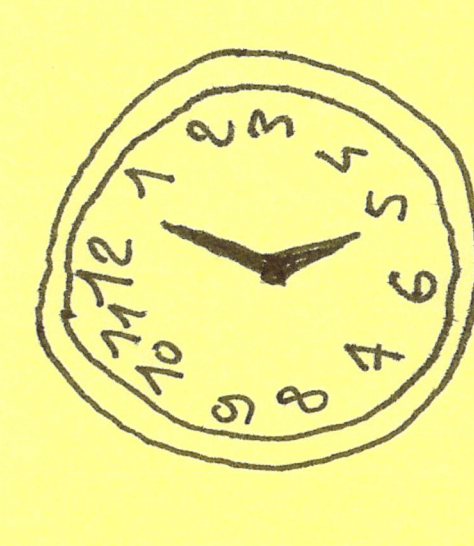

WE ARE IN 2212, TIME HAS NOT CHANGED

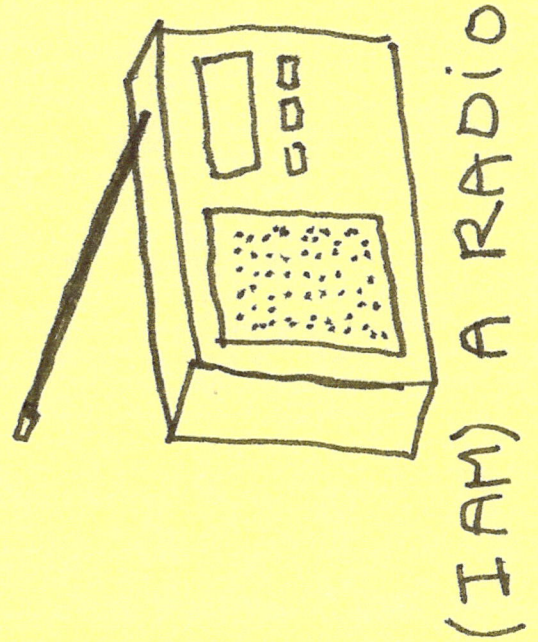

(I AM) A RADIO

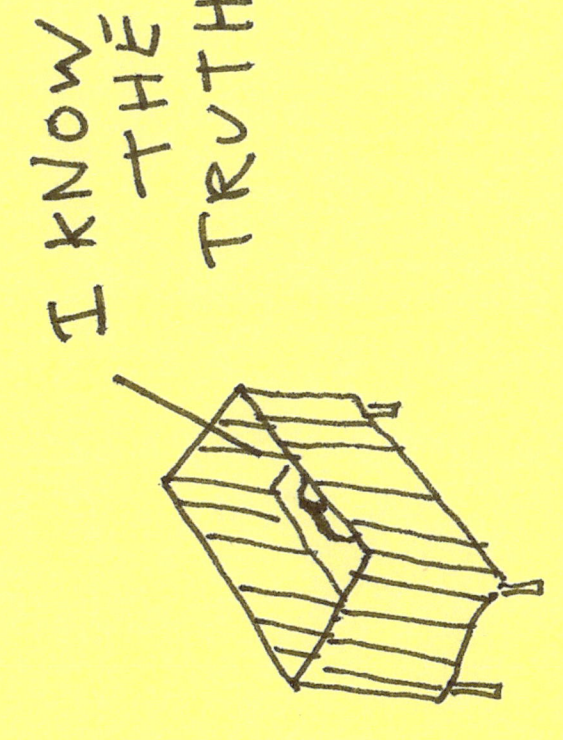

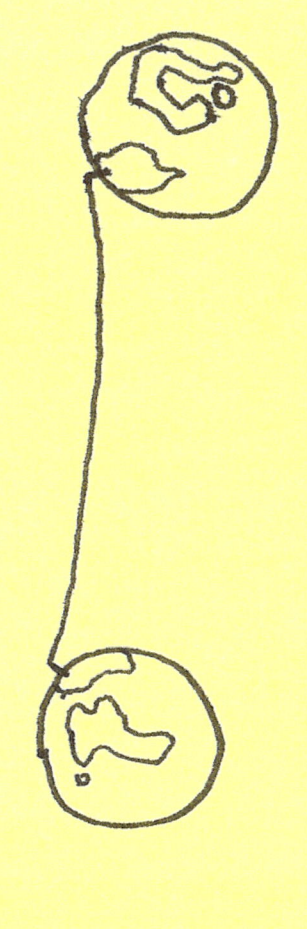

I PUT A WIRE SO WE CAN COMMUNICATE